ETERNAL THREADS

by *[signature: Patterson]*

Patty Sue Patton

*In Pagosa Springs,
I am known as
Patty Tellerson*

authorHOUSE™

1663 LIBERTY DRIVE, SUITE 200
BLOOMINGTON, INDIANA 47403
(800) 839-8640
WWW.AUTHORHOUSE.COM

First published by AuthorHouse 03/03/05

ISBN: 1-4208-3351-0 (sc)

Printed in the United States of America
Bloomington, Indiana

This book is printed on acid-free paper.

Dedicated to my loving husband
and life-time partner,

Bob J. Tillerson

And the three blessed souls God
trusted to our care who have in
turn blessed our lives.

and

In loving memory of my parents,

Emma McInnis
Ray Vernon Patton

Contents

Preface...ix

Introduction.. 1

Childhood Journey 11

Period of Discovery 17

Who Am I?.. 27

    Maternal Influence 31

    Paternal Influence 35

Discussion 41

    The Light 43

    Living Within the Light 47

    Suffer the Little Children 52

Conclusion 57

Epilogue 69

References.. 73

PREFACE

This is a record of my personal journey's experience up to now. Special appreciation to both Manfred Barthel and Elaine Pagels for their research and writings which gave me the confidence to examine my journey in depth.

In today's world, many young people have no church affiliation and I have wondered why this is, for I know many who are good folks, doing good things with their lives. Through the research of both Barthel and Pagels, I believe I have found the answer: organized churches today have made religion so complex through the "overdoing" of Bible studies and other requirements, that many have become confused and thus, see no need to participate.

There is a common thread, extending back to the Essene community prior to Christ, repeated in the Old and New Testaments and strongly emphasized in the newly discovered Secret Gospel of Thomas that simplifies religious practice through individual responsibility:

"Love the Lord your God with all your heart, with all your mind, and with all your soul and your neighbor as yourself."

If we strive to obey those commandments, then all other rules become insignificant. So, I pray that this record of my journey will help others to recognize that religion is very personal, that God has given to each of us an eternal soul to nurture along its journey and that organized religion is not necessarily a requirement.

Now, I do not wish to cast disfavor on those active in organized churches, for it is important to recognize the value of close relationships between those of like practice. The organized churches serve as a social strengthening as they join with others to serve the needs of their community. However, no church should be a detriment to one's personal responsibilities or attempt to pass judgement on any other group of faith. **What really matters is how we live within what we do** rather than emphasis upon what we do. Do we love God totally and do we love our neighbor, our co-worker, our employees, our boss, and even those outside our close circle, as ourselves? If we live within those commandments, then the purpose of worship with like believers should be to provide strength.

I appreciate Elaine Pagels' statement in her book, <u>Beyond Belief:</u>

> *"Orthodoxy tends to distrust our capacity to make discriminations and insists on making them for us. Given the notorious human capacity for self-deception we can, to an extent, thank the church for this. Many of us, wishing to be spared hard work, gladly accept what tradition teaches."*

It most surely is an unfortunate tragedy that the emphasis on organized church dogmas has resulted in our present-day division among communities of the faithful. Most surely this is sad in the eyes of God, who loves all.

Again, Elaine Pagels states so clearly:

> *". . . the fact that we have no simple answer does not mean that we can evade the question. We have seen the hazards— even the terrible harm —that sometimes*

result from unquestioning acceptance of religious authority. Most of us, sooner or later, find that at critical points in our lives, we must strike out on our own to make a path where none exists. As Jesus said, 'Seek and you shall find'."

The Secret Gospel of Thomas states:

"If you bring forth what is within you, what you bring forth will save you."

When Thomas questioned Jesus as to how he should live, Jesus answered:

"The Kingdom is inside of you and outside of you. When you come to know yourselves, then you will be known and you will see that it is you who are the children of the living Father. But if you will not know yourselves, you dwell in poverty and it is you who are that poverty."

Thomas then asked Jesus:

"How can we know ourselves?"

Jesus answered:

> *"Find out first where you came from and go back and take your place in the beginning. . . Blessed is the one who came into being before he came into being."*

Yes, we are blessed when we recognize that the soul within us, the eternal part made in God's image, was a Being before we were born.

Thus, the purpose of recording my journey is to inspire others to discover the power of their personal "Light", accept God's guidance along their journey and live a joyous life filled with hope when their darkness becomes light.

INTRODUCTION

"Though outwardly we are wasting away, yet inwardly we are being renewed day by day."

(The Apostle Paul)

THE LORD,

By **wisdom** hath founded the earth;
By **understanding** hath he
establised the heavens.

IN ALL THY WAYS,

Acknowledge Him and He shall
direct thy paths.

(Proverbs 3: 6 & 9)

Throughout my life, I have been uncomfortable with various interpretations of religion—could never find my own "niche", so to speak. While my faith has been strong, mainstream theology has never held my interest as much as with some active Christians.

I have enjoyed the fellowship of church membership throughout my life and have been active in serving needs in the community outside of the organized church.

Raised as Christian, I was not exposed to other religious practices until I became interested some years ago. Most bothersome to me is why does any one organized faith have a right to claim perfection when there is just one God who created all of us? Who decided that religion must be so complicated? Were not the writers of the Bible stories writing within the social and political context of their times? Does the organized church impose too much study on its members for its own survival? Does individual faith have respect amidst the adopted dogma of the organized churches?

The First Century writings unearthed in Upper Egypt near Nag Hammadi in 1945 certainly lend support to some of these questions. The discovery included the Secret Gospel of Thomas, which had been suppressed by those who adopted the books of the Bible and considered it heresy, as it was in conflict with the writings in the Gospel of John, which were more "in tune" with those of Mathew, Mark and Luke with some difference while the Gospel of Thomas included a major difference, which you will see.

It seems that the denial of the Thomas writings by scholars limited Western Christian theology, both intellectually and spiritually—a true example of political interference with spiritual truth.

Having lost my parents when I was young, I came to realize how much they and my children had missed. My children did not know me as well as they should without exposure to my parents as their grandparents. So, this desire began my search for my soul's journey.

As a child, I could not understand how "we" were created in God's image when everyone looked different—how could God look like so many? Then, of course, I came to conclude that it is our soul that he created in his image and it is that part of us that is immortal. God gave us a body to house our soul and a mind to communicate with him; thus, mind, body and soul all three make up our earthly Being. While our soul is nurtured by our parents and others around us, it is through prayer that God gives it guidance and purpose. It is our responsibility to connect with God through prayer and, I believe, when our earthly life is gone, God takes our soul, gives it rest, and in time, returns it to a new body, to a newborn within the family, to continue its journey for His purpose.

Apostle Paul, in II Corinthians, chapter 4, verses 16-18, states:

> *"though outwardly we are wasting away, yet inwardly we are being renewed day by day. For our Light and momentary troubles are achieving for us an eternal glory that far outweighs them all. So, we fix our eyes not on what is seen but on what is unseen. For what is seen is temporary but what is unseen is eternal."*

When Thomas asked Jesus when will the end come? Jesus answered:

> *"What you look forward to has already come, but you do not recognize it. It will not come by waiting for it. It will not be a matter of saying, 'Here it is' or 'There it is'. Rather, the Kingdom of the Father is spread out upon the earth and people do not see it."*

I have long believed that heaven is right here on earth, that every time we do something good for someone else, we experience a "little bit of heaven". Those things need not be big or great but simply a warm smile, a caring touch, a sparkle in the eye, encouraging words— many times, so simple that we are unaware of the good we have done; however, there are times when we are blessed to see the results of God's goodness done through his guidance and use of our souls. We never know at the beginning of a day what lies ahead, who will we encounter along the journey, and what will be expected of us. However, if we begin that day's journey with a prayer for his guidance, He will provide.

I will now share the spiritual experience of my father's last days. Soon after my mother's death, he was diagnosed with cancer and his prognosis was, at the most, three years. He told me that my mother had appeared in his bedroom door one night to tell him not to worry, that everything would be OK. This caused me to believe that following death, we become spiritual Beings to continue God's purpose until we are returned within a human body. Upon my Dad's final admission to the hospital, the physician counseled that he would soon lapse into a coma and that death was probably weeks away. Knowing my Dad's wishes, I prayed by his bedside that God please come and take him, not to have him linger. The next morning, he said to me:

"Just one more day and this will be over."

During the early morning hours of the next day, I became aware that Christ had entered his room and taken his soul away—left behind was simply his earthly body, which lived a few more hours. Did I know exactly when Christ came for him? No, I just experienced what had occurred. My prayer was answered.

Influences beyond one's self play a part in our journey. God protects the souls of those who continue to recognize his goodness and ask for his guidance through hard times and good times. In my review of the translated writings among the new discoveries, I believe that God gave to us the means to reproduce our bodies and at the time of our first breath, he gave us an eternal soul, created in his image, to continue his purpose through generations.

I hope my story will enlighten others to look deeply within themselves for personal understanding and recognition of God within. My journey has been fascinating!

CHILDHOOD JOURNEY

". . .in every worthy life, that which has really left the greatest measure of good, has been its ministry of kindness."

(Reverend Miller, 1905)

I have no recollection of being focused upon material things as a child. Oh yes, I wanted that certain doll for Christmas and I always got it! But, as to being aware of things that represented wealth, I don't believe I ever was. I loved my parents, my baby sister, and playing make-believe with my brother.

My soul was shaped by events surrounding me. Of course, there was the Great Depression followed by World War II that required sacrifice of all. However, I believe it was my mother's illness and my father's kindness that shaped my soul during my childhood years. Always affectionate, my mother's endearing smile and outward friendliness never left her, even as she struggled with the mental and physical effects of her disease which went undiagnosed for many years.

My grandmother McInnis lived with us until I was about 14 years of age. She was a cheerful person, despite a life filled with tragedies. She and my Dad were good friends and I believe she was a sense of encouragement and enlightenment for him. When she died, I took her place in mother's life, which by then had become mostly home-centered as she had dropped out of all outside interests, due to mental depression from a slow-growing brain tumor. During my teenage years and throughout high school, it was normal for me to come home from school, clean up the kitchen from breakfast and lunch. Then Daddy would arrive home and often, it would be for us to get something started for dinner and of course, afterwards, we did the dishes together. Thus, I was unable to have friends during my teenage years—only dates, as I was needed at home. What is interesting, though, is that I really never minded! I was happy with my life. So, perhaps this was the start of my soul's journey, for caring for others has been my joy and still is!

This devotion to my mother continued even after my marriage, for my focus was doing things to have her happy. So, again, I had no time to be with friends my own age but I didn't mind, for it had always been that way.

During my Dad's many hospitalizations, I expressed alarm at the daily cost of his room, but he answered:

"It's OK—I am meeting the cost of one whose room is in the basement, who has no money."

He received many floral gifts during his many stays and he would enjoy each for a few hours, then would have the staff take them down to those basement rooms to brighten their days. He truly lived "love thy neighbor as thyself".

My Dad was not much for the organized church and if one looks back at his ancestry, it is understandable. His young life was the "cowboy way". Both his father and his grandfather were cowboys and yes, they had religion. They loved nature and nature's ways and were open-minded and fair in business. My Dad was committed to community service and showed special concern for the welfare of his employees and for the wives of those called to serve during World War II. He read extensively—the Bible, World Philosophy, etc.—had God in his life daily and when he needed God, God was the there for him.

PERIOD OF DISCOVERY

"Be ye doers of the word"

(Book of James)

When the youngest child left for college, I began to have time to reflect and felt an emptiness— missed my parents, wished they could have seen my children grow up and how wonderful they had become. This led me to wonder about my parents' past, what shaped their lives?

In my first book of Threads, I wrote the following, regarding the task:

> *"This search for answers has been far more challenging and rewarding than I ever imagined at the start. Feelings and instincts I have felt throughout my life have been given purpose through this search. I felt 'shoved' into this some years ago, walking along the bayou in Houston, Texas. It was then that the title 'Threads' came to mind and I began, over time, to develop ideas that I knew were being placed in my mind by the Almighty. I knew I did not have the wisdom or ability to do this alone, but it continued to haunt and excite me and finally, when I retired from the world of making a living. I felt a strong commitment to take this task on. At first, I thought it was simply a matter of locating my ancestors*

and writing a few facts down in a book. However, as time went by, I felt He expected more of me than that and I began to recognize that the real task He had given me was to use my findings to strengthen the spirituality of my children and my children's children—for how can they receive guidance from those they have never seen?"

So, the first thing I did was develop an overall philosophy for my books. In 1991, I wrote in my first book:

"Threads. . . that make up the very fabric of our Being; the strengths handed down from generation to generation that give purpose to those who follow. These threads, carefully selected by our Maker, are of varied hues to give us balance of beauty and purpose. Families have obligations known only to God and the threads continued throughout generations are those important to His Kingdom on Earth as well as in Heaven. You may never know greatness during your lifetime, but your contributions are important to His Plan. To find

true happiness in this life, we must alert ourselves to these strengths and obligations—accept them as true gifts, be forever thankful for them, and never let ourselves forget that our talents, our abilities, and everything we own belong to God—He has entrusted them to us to be used wisely and without greed. . . Be alert and proud. Pursue your life with faith and confidence, and despite a few flaws, your threads will become part of an original masterpiece of God's work through which others will come to know Him. "

What surprises me now is the depth in meaning of my written philosophy of 1991 when one compares it to the translations of the Secret Gospel of Thomas! Surely it was God's guidance!

Also, during the research for my first book, I discovered the little book, <u>The Beauty of Kindness</u>. among my Grandmother Josie's things. It contained a sermon, apparently very important to her. The Presbyterian minister, Reverend Miller, wrote in 1905:

*"Some of us, if we were to try to sum up
the total of our usefulness, would name a
few large things we have done—the giving
of money to some benevolent object, the
starting of some good work which has
grown into strength, the writing of a
book which has made us widely known,
the winning of honor in some service to
our community or country. But in every
worthy life, that which has really left
the greatest measure of goodness has
been its ministry of kindness. . . where
we have gone, day after day, if we have
simply been kind to everyone, we have
left blessings in the world which, in
their sum, far exceed the good wrought,
the help imparted, and the cheer given
by the few large conspicuous things of
which we think and speak with pride."*

Reverend Miller continues:

*". . . Many of those to whom the world
owes the most, wrought obscurely, in
poverty, ofttimes sacrificing themselves,
toiling, struggling, suffering, in order
to perfect their invention or discovery.
They saw nothing great or splendid in*

what they were doing. In many cases, their lives seemed failures, for they were only pioneers and achieved nothing themselves. Others came after them and carried to perfection what they had striven in vain to accomplish. Today the things they dreamed of but never realized are among the world's finest achievements, its most useful inventions. ... born in their brain and made possible through their dream and self-denying devotion."

The "Eternal Soul" at work?

Since discovering the value of daily prayers for my soul, I have been able to live with confidence, knowing that He is in my life and guiding me in all that I do. He has provided me with the right words of encouragement to others I am called to help. Many times, words I would not have thought to say, came just the same.

During my years of caring for folks while serving on the ambulance, I often prayed silently during the transport without the patient's knowledge.

Two outstanding examples of the result of my prayers, I offer here.

There was a fellow who would come to town from time to time and wash dishes or the such to earn a little money, which he would then spend at the local bar. The ambulance service was called on several occasions when he would be found unconscious from consumption. I had transported him several times and on that certain day, he recognized me from the past. As he became able to converse, he began to visit about family, etc. and he put his arms out for a hug. I told him that if he would be good, I would give him a hug when we arrived at the hospital. He answered, "but you are such a kind lady". Now, I don't know how I came to answer him in this way but believe it was God working through me. I thanked him and then stated, "You know, there is a very kind person inside of you but no one can know that person because of the way you abuse your body." He became very pensive, as though this was a new thought he had never heard, and he remained silent and pensive the rest of the hour-long transport. Yes, when we arrived, I kept my promise and gave him that hug. What is interesting is that, to my knowledge, we were never again called to pick him up. Did my words open a new door for him. Perhaps he discovered his inner Light? Perhaps his counselors were able to succeed? I will never know, of course.

Then, there was that very distraught young lady—so much so that we had to restrain her for the transport. She was screaming and kicking and we were unable to calm her. However, now and then, she would become exhausted and take a break. During one of her breaks, I said a silent prayer for her in which I asked God to wrap his arms around her and support her with his love. What happened next was quite surprising! All of a sudden, she looked up and said, "I see angels, angels all around me". She remained calm the rest of the trip and we were able to remove the restraints.

When I pray for guidance, God never lets me down.

WHO AM I?

Thomas asked Jesus: "How can we know ourselves?"

Jesus answered: "Find out first where you came from and go back and take your place in the beginning. . . Blessed is the one who came into being before he came into being."

I ask, who nourished the souls of my parents, who in turn, nourished mine? In the Introductions to my two books, Threads I and Threads II, written in 1991 and 1992, I described their religious histories. In the first book, which is about my mother, I wrote about the religious symbol used on the death notice of my great-grandfather, Frank Xavier Fredrick—that the cross signifies death and the crown, everlasting life, mentioned in the Book of James:

Regarding trials and tribulations. . . such testing of one's faith develops perseverance, which is of utmost importance to become a mature, complete individual.

Regarding wisdom. . . if we find ourselves without the wisdom to face a challenge, we should ask God for the wisdom needed, as He gives generously to all. However, he also states that one must ask and accept with faith—that doubters find themselves like a wave, blown and tossed by the wind.

Regarding works and faith. . . both are necessary when he says, "For the body

> *without the spirit is dead, so faith without works is dead also".*

It appears that James questions the honesty of one who claims to believe but fails to live the faith.

Then, in the second book, I described my father's history, which revealed their obedience to God and allegiance to country:

> *"One nation under God, indivisible, with liberty and justice for all. This is the story of a family, your family, strongly dedicated to the ideals of freedom and justice for all. Through obedience to God and allegiance to country, they were supporters of change so long as it showed promise of a better life for most, opposed to a few. This story will make you proud, for it has become part of you."*

Through my research, I discovered the "why" of my inner self, my soul. Here is a very brief history of my parents' ancestors.

Maternal Influence

My research took me back to France, in the early time of the Reformation Movement. My great-great-Uncle had become a Jesuit Priest. It was apparent that the family was dedicated to the Jesuit Movement, as my great-great-grandfather was named Frank Xavier Friderick and he also named his son, my great-grandfather, Frank Xavier Friderick (changed to Fredrick when he immigrated to America). Young "F.X." was sent to live with his Jesuit Priest Uncle at an early age because the family believed he would gain the best education from him, for the Jesuits have been known always as the best teachers, scientists, and mathematicians as well as for their missionary work. The importance of carrying the name "Xavier" forward most surely was to honor one they truly admired and believed in, St. Francis Xavier. In his book, The Jesuits: History and Legend of the Society of Jesus, Barthel describes him in this way:

> *"Francis Xavier, the patron saint of all Catholic missions overseas, has been called 'the most important Christian evangelist since Paul' which is high praise indeed. It is certainly fair to say*

> *that his travels took him farther, among more different peoples, than any other missionary since Paul. . . the Society of Jesus was intended from the beginning to be an order, unlike any of its predecessors, in which the emphasis was very much on the active side of things rather than the purely contemplative. . . the Jesuits did not wear a distinctive habit. . . they did not chant the liturgy or participate in communal prayer of any kind. (Prayer and meditation was and is strictly an individual matter with the Jesuits). The Jesuit's cure of souls is not sharply defined and his activity is certainly not restricted to the parish and the pulpit. The boundaries of his parish extend to wherever the soothing influence of the Church is needed, and the Jesuit's pulpit might be the roof of a camper, a scaffold on a construction site, or the speaker's dais at the U.N. General Assembly. "*

My mother's paternal side was also strong in the nurturing of her soul, despite her father's early death when she was just age 15. Her father's family immigrated from Scotland to Canada where his ancestral father was a wagon-maker.

He later built cars for the railroad and taught his son, Frank McInnis, the trade. They were Presbyterian and of special interest is the fact that the Presbyterian faith was also founded by a French Reformer, John Calvin, who attended the same college as the founder of the Society of Jesus! Calvin's academy in Geneva, Switzerland, closely paralleled the constitution of the Society of Jesus. Both emphasized the importance of education, discipline, and freedom of religious expression.

When my Catholic grandmother Josie met and fell in love with my Presbyterian grandfather in the 1890s, the Catholic Orthodoxy had grown to the degree that intermarriage between Catholic and Protestant was all but forbidden. However, the past history of these two families, whose religious practice coincided in the beginning, had continued their steady, unrelenting tolerance and their marriage was embraced by Josie's Catholic parents and she became a Presbyterian!

Frank McInnis was very religious. He supported Josie with love and understanding. His early death was due to trauma. Written inside the Bible he used, in his own handwriting, are written three Scriptures that must have been his guide to living:

> *"Proverbs 22:1: A good name is more desirable than great riches; to be highly esteemed is better than silver or gold".*

> *"Corr 10:31: So whether you eat or drink or whatever you do, do it all for the glory of God."*

> *"Mt 6:21: For where your treasure is, there your heart will be also".*

Paternal Influence

My father's history carried me back to the 1600s and revealed my patriotism and strong need to do community service. In this country, "one nation under God", citizens were guaranteed freedom from government-controlled religious practice and thus I strongly believe it to be Un-American for a political candidate to use organized religion for personal political gain.

The Pattons were Scotch-Irish and proud leaders, always dedicated to freedom. They were organizers everywhere they went and known for their honesty, generosity and understanding towards their fellow man. They were strong Presbyterians and followers of John Calvin, whose Christianity was described in my second book of Threads:

> *"He calls us to be strong and that we should relate our entire life activities to God's guidance; to be free because those who are bound to God's Will from day to day most surely cannot bind their conscience and life to man's Will; and that we carry our Christian works out into the world, to be leaders of great*

principle, governed by God and dedicated to truthfulness and righteousness."

The Patton history is filled with risk, strength, patriotism and tenacity in the face of tragedy. My father's Dad had been raised as a cowboy, lived as a cowboy in his younger years and later entered business, studied and practiced law, and was elected to several political offices over his lifetime. He welcomed settlers into the Texas Panhandle, where he had worked as a cowboy for many years and was later elected Mayor of Amarillo, Texas., where his major source of income was from his wholesale liquor business. When the County was voted "dry", he had to move and start over as a business man. However, he never expressed bitterness but rather urged the public to support the new law. An example of his character was noted by Resolution and signed by the City Aldermen in accepting his resignation as Mayor:

"Whereas the honored Mayor of our city, James H. Patton, has decided to move to California, and has tendered his resignation as Mayor of Amarillo. . . that in accepting his resignation we do so with regrets. We who know

James H. Patton and have served the city with him realize that in him the city has had a model Mayor. We know that he has conscientiously given the city a progressive and business-like administration and that Amarillo has been benefitted under his wise Mayorship. Be it further resolved that by Mayor Patton's moving to California, Amarillo not only loses a most able officer of city affairs, but our citizens lost a good man who is a gentleman in every sense of the word, a man who is public-spirited, who is fair in business, high-minded and of clean character, and who never turns a deaf ear to charity and that we hope God's blessing will follow him and his to their new home."

This was just the beginning of a life filled with tragedy, financial loss and eventually failing health. However, he never allowed himself to become bitter, remained interested in his fellow man and continued his pleasant ways.

My Dad's mother came from a needy background, her father a Baptist preacher who moved around a lot. Her insecure childhood had not prepared her for the disappointments they endured and the final "blow" was the Great Depression when he lost all of his real estate holdings and their lives went from wealthy to poor. Her happy spirit never recovered.

I also provided my children with their father's history as recorded in <u>Threads III and Threads IV</u>, as they must seek the destiny of their own souls. I am very proud of their journeys and know they will grow over time. In writing <u>Threads IV</u>, which is a record of their childhoods, I stated the following, based upon my belief of life as taught by my parents:

> *"I recall a comment made by my father's attorney following his death: 'Your parents have left you a rich inheritance.' Was he referring to material wealth? No, for my parents were far from wealthy. Rather, he was referring to character wealth—the examples left by my parents and their ancestors. . . Your heritage is indeed rich in character. Be proud and pursue your dreams with determination and thankfulness, building character in everyone you touch along the way—use your inheritance to give encouragement*

to others whose heritage is not so rich—it is through sharing that our riches bring us the greatest happiness!"

DISCUSSION

"If you really keep the law found in Scripture 'Love your neighbor as yourself', you are doing right."

(James 2:8)

The Light

Manfred Barthel, in his book, <u>What the Bible Really Says,</u> writes that through the discovery of the Dead Sea Scrolls in 1956, came the "uncovering" of the ancient community of Qumran near the city of Jerusalem. This community was home to the religious sect known as the Essenes, who existed prior to the birth of Christ.

Interpretations of the spirituality of the Essenes have been found to have a "kinship" to many writings in the New Testament of the Bible. Thus, God's spirituality was with us even prior to Christ. The Essenes stood up to the Romans, fought and died for their faith. An account left by Flavius Josephus, a Roman student of the Essenes, described their beliefs in this way:

> *"It is their unalterable conviction that the flesh is subject to decay and that the material body is ephemeral, but that the soul, being immortal, endures forever."*

So, one must assume that even in ancient times, God's image was immortal within all.

Reading from the King James Version of the Bible, we are told the following:

> *". . . the Lord formed man of the dust of the ground and breathed into his nostrils the breath of life and man became a living soul."* (Book of Genesis)

Then, reading from the Book of John, we are told that all things were made by God and without him nothing was made—that in him was life and his life was the light of all men. The Book of John 20:30, further states that:

> *"many other signs of truth did Jesus in the presence of his disciples, which are not written in this book. . ."*

So, who is Jesus? Both John and Thomas state that Jesus directed them towards the beginning of time, to the creation account in Genesis rather than the end of time as stated in Mathew, Mark and Luke. John and Thomas both identify Jesus with the divine light that came into being *"in the beginning. . ."* Both state that the primordial light connects Jesus with the entire universe, since, as John 1:3-10, says:

"all things were made through the word"

Mathew, Mark and Luke identify Jesus as God's human agent while both John and Thomas characterize him as God's own light in human form. An example of this is recorded in John 3:21:

". . . . whoever lives by the truth comes into the light so that what he has done has been done through God."

Where John and Thomas disagree is that John states that Jesus alone brings divine light to the world—that we experience God only through the divine light embodied in Jesus. Thomas, on the other hand, states that the <u>divine light Jesus embodied is shared by all humanity</u> since we are all made *"in the image of God'—that the "light" in Jesus is within each of us to be discovered.*

Pagels states that John was written in the midst of controversy to defend some views of Jesus and oppose others and thus, was the beginning of the effect of political views on "acceptable" Christian theology of the New Testament. She writes that, for Christians in later generations, the Gospel of John helped provide a foundation for a unified church, which Thomas, with the emphasis on each person's search for God, did not. However, I ask: Did the Gospel of John truly result in a unified church? Today? I think not!

In summary, what John opposed includes what the Gospel of Thomas teaches—that God's light shines not only in Jesus but, potentially, in everyone. According to the Gospel of Thomas, Jesus encouraged us to know God through our own divine capacity, since we are created in God's image "from the beginning".

Living Within the Light

When Jesus' followers asked:

"Who will be our leader when you are gone?"

The Gospel of Thomas provides this reply:

"No matter where you are, you are to go to James the Just, for whose sake heaven and earth came into being."

Of course, he was referring to James, the brother of Christ. This carries for me very special importance since my Jesuit ancestors placed much emphasis upon the writings of James. Two quotes I offer here regarding one's practice of faith:

"Everyone should be quick to listen, slow to speak and slow to become angry, for man's anger does not bring about the righteous life that God desires. Therefore, get rid of all moral filth and the evil that is prevalent and humbly accept the word planted in you which can save you" (James 1:19-21)

Then, in James 2:8:

> *"If you really keep the law found in Scripture: 'Love your neighbor as yourself', you are doing right".*

Barthel, in his book <u>The History of the Jesuits</u>, reveals the humbleness of the Jesuit teachings:

> *"One should present one's self to the world not as oneself but in imitation of Jesus Christ by means of one's service to mankind."*

Additional support of the need to practice humbleness is recorded in Mathew 6:5-7:

> *"When you pray, do not be like the hypocrites, for they love to pray standing in the synagogues and on the street corners to be seen by men. . . but go into your room close your door, and pray to your Father who is unseen. . . and when you pray, do not keep on babbling, like pagans, for they think they will be heard because of their many words."*

I have never been one to appreciate lengthy public prayers. Silent meditation has always been more beneficial to me. During my parents' illnesses, I began to appreciate what I call "being God-conscious". During those busy years, I did not take time for daily prayers as such—three little ones to care for meant many demands to meet; but I did talk to God while in my car or as I cleaned my house or did the ironing. He was "in my life" every day. So, even today, I continue to be "God-conscious" and have received many of the ideas for this book during my morning walks and often I awake in the early morning with a new thought placed while I slept!

There are many references that bear witness to Christ's commandment to love our neighbors as ourselves, starting with the translations from the Qumran texts of the Essenes and included in Barthel's book, <u>What the Bible Really Says:</u>

> "... that poverty, chastity and humility were the first prerequisites for a life of righteousness, that we should love our enemies as well as our neighbors..."

Then, in the Old Testament Book of Leviticus, Chapter 19, verse 18, we find:

> *"Never seek revenge or bear a grudge against anyone, but love your neighbor as yourself".*

Then, the Apostle Paul states so clearly in the Book of Romans, chapter 13, verses 8-9:

> *"Let no debt remain outstanding except the continuing debt to love one another, for he who loves his fellowman has fulfilled the law. . . whatever other commandments there may be are summed up in this one rule: 'Love your neighbor as yourself.' Love does no harm to its neighbor. Therefore, love is the fulfillment of the law."*

So, in summary, how do we "live the light"? Love the Lord our God with all our heart, with all our mind and with all our soul and our neighbor as ourselves–clear and simple! Then, in the book of First Corinthians, Chapter 1, verses 1-8, Paul defines heavenly love in this way:

"If I speak in tongues of men and of angels, but have not love, I am only a resounding gong or a clanging cymbal. If I have the gift of prophecy and can fathom all mysteries and all knowledge, and if I have a faith that can move mountains, but have not love, I am nothing. If I give all I possess to the poor and surrender my body to the flames, but have not love, I gain nothing. Love is patient, love is kind, it does not envy, it does not boast, it is not proud. It is not rude, it is not self-seeking, it is not easily angered. It keeps no record of wrongs. Love does not delight in evil but rejoices with the truth. It always protects, always trusts, always hopes, always perseveres."

Suffer the Little Children

We have no idea who God has placed in our care, but one thing is clear–there are obligations that come with that sweet little gift. Barthel, in his book, <u>What the Bible Really Says,</u> points out that prior to the time of Christ, people were quite indifferent to their children and provided little guidance.

However, Christ's famous proclamation recorded in the Book of Mathew, Chapter 19, verse 14:

> *"Let the children come to me and do not hinder them for the Kingdom of heaven belongs to such as these"*

changed this attitude for future generations. Jesus went even further, as stated in the Book of Mark, Chapter 9, verse 37:

> *"Whoever welcomes one of these little children in my name welcomes me; and whoever welcomes me does not welcome me but the one who sent me."*

So, this most certainly supports that God's light is in each of us, only to be discovered.

My grandmother Josie had saved, among her things, a written legend by Isabel Graham that describes the attitude by which she lived; how a need might go unnoticed. I believe this describes very well the value of a child:

"There was a monk who knelt continually in his cell and prayed. He had made a vow that none should see his face until he had looked upon the face of Christ. So, his devotions were unbroken. The birds sang by his cell window and the children played without, but the monk heeded not either the children or the birds. In the absorption of his soul, in its passion for the face of Christ, he was oblivious to all earthly things.

One morning, he seemed to hear a spirit-voice saying that his prayer to see the Blessed One should be answered that day. He was very glad and made special preparations for the coming of the vision. There was a gentle knocking at his door, by and by, and the voice of a child was

*heard pleading to be fed and taken in.
Her feet were cold, her clothing was
thin. . . But the monk was so intent on the
coming of the vision that he could not
pause to minister to any human needs.
Evening drew on, the place became
dreary, the tapers burned low. Why
was the vision so long in appearing?
Then, with bitter grief, the monk heard
the answer that the vision had already
come, had lingered at his door, and then,
unwelcome, had sobbed and turned
away. Jesus had come in a little child,
cold and hungry, had knocked, called,
waited, and grieved, had gone."*

So, what is our responsibility as parents? Is
it merely to recreate ourselves or does it
carry other responsibilities? Remember, that
according to the story in Genesis, the minute
that little creation takes it first breath, God
gives it a soul (his "Light" within) to continue
its journey for his purpose. From what we are
learning from the translations of the Gospel of
Thomas, this soul is God's image within that
newborn and it is our obligation to love, guide
and encourage it throughout the path of life
to fulfill His purpose, unknown to us. A big

assignment! However, if we pray for guidance along the way, acknowledging the strengths and ambitions of the child with encouragement, we will do well.

It is good for the child to learn about the stories in the Bible—the bad and the good, for that is history. However, we cannot rely only on that, but rather acknowledge the "Light" that is within and encourage goodness in all things. Teach them the value of silent prayer, the recognition of God within.

I have found it interesting to observe the two sets of identical twins in my family. They are born from the same womb, mirror images of each other; however, just hours into life, differences in personality begin to show up. Could this be the individual souls provided by God that are unseen? Has to be, for what else would cause them to be so different? Parents must then respect and encourage their individual interests, while providing spiritual nourishment throughout their childhood. Spiritual nourishment requires nothing material, of course; but we must care for their bodies to provide a healthy environment for their soul and encourage their minds to learn all they can to prepare them for the journey they will take.

In closing, I recall a sweet childhood prayer taught to me by my mother. Its origin must go back generations and if one really thinks of its meaning, perhaps it began with the Gospel of Thomas:

"Now I lay me down to sleep,
I pray the Lord my soul to keep,
That should I die before I wake,
I pray the Lord my soul to take.

Think about it—even the young child is taught that the soul within belongs to God and is precious; so, God, please take care of it for me!

Interesting!

CONCLUSION

"You are the light of the world. . .
Let your light shine before men,
that they may see your good deeds
and praise your Father in heaven."

(Mathew 5:14 and 16)

History records the activities of two Christian missionaries of the Second Century, which appear to reflect the overall emphasis of the writings in the Secret Gospel of Thomas. Elaine Pagels describes these in her book, <u>Beyond Belief.</u> There was Iranius, who led a Christian group in Gaul. Pagel states that:

> *"He took no money, practiced spiritual healing, helped those in need throughout the Empire of Egypt, Antioch, Carthage and Rome; that he became frustrated that none of the writers of the Gospels could agree and was concerned with the separations into many denominations of believers. . . that if anyone gives himself up to them like a little sheep, and follows their practice, such a person is so elated that he imagines he has already entered within the 'fullness of God' and goes about strutting around with a superior expression on his face, with all the pomposity of a cock."*

Do you know anyone like that? Then Pagels describes the African convert and Christian spokesman, Tertullian, in this way:

"He gave money voluntarily to support orphans, fed and supplied meds to prisoners and even bought coffins and dug graves for the poor and criminal who otherwise would have been left lying. He stated 'There is no buying or selling in what belongs to God. On a certain day, if he likes, puts in a small gift but only if he wants to and only if he is able, for there is no compulsion, everything is voluntary'."

Pagels states that his generosity attracted crowds of newcomers to Christianity, for both Jews and Christians at that time believed that God, who created humankind, evoked love, e.g., "What God requires is that human beings love one another and offer help even, or especially, to the neediest". Those who practiced this were known as "peculiar Christians", that what marked them in the eyes of their enemies was their lovingkindness.

The profound difference between the writings of Thomas and those of the other gospels is that Secret Message whispered to Thomas by Christ, that Christ's divine light is within each and every one of us which makes all of humanity children of God the Father, rather than Christ alone.

Thomas refused to share this message with the rest, stating that they would stone him to death and of course, one must believe also that the message would have been attacked, discredited and destroyed. That secret message is the defining difference between Thomas and the others. Thomas could not risk its destruction. So, it was written and preserved to be recently discovered.

The discovery of this very important Gospel certainly alters one's perception of God and I believe it is of special significance that it is now being translated and made public. There is so much division all over the world between the various methods of worship–perhaps this will serve to unite all under the praise and worship of our one and only Father, God. From Thomas, we learn that Christ came to teach us how to live, to demonstrate God's love and forgiveness, and to alert us that through his teachings and sacrifice, our own souls are on an eternal journey for God's purpose—that our journey is personal, between us and God alone.

Today, there are many who write, sell, and distribute books all over the world proclaiming just one religious philosophy, putting forth a form of "religious fear" in order to gain followers who have not discovered the loving God. This is sad and the writings in the Secret Book of Thomas most certainly make that invalid.

Manfred Bartel, in his book <u>What the Bible Really Says,</u> states that many passages in the Book of Revelations have so many possible meanings that they come very close to having no meaning at all. No one has been able to fully understand the message of those words. However, the Secret Book of Thomas proclaims the value and strength of God's love in this way:

> *". . . joy to those who receive from the Father the grace of knowing him. . . those who receive this Gospel no longer think of God as petty, nor harsh, nor wrathful. . . but as a being without evil, loving, full of tranquility, gracious and all knowing."*

Thomas further states:

"human existence apart from God is a nightmare but by discovering God's presence here and now, the terror lessens as his spirit extends a hand, lifts us up, supports us in all things and finally restores the soul."

Regarding the importance of daily prayer, some might ask: "How can you believe that God really speaks to you? Does he have a voice? Of course not! God is spiritual, he opens our minds to his wisdom and provides us with confidence to make difficult decisions; he opens our hearts to his love to provide us the strength to rise from darkness to light during trying times. Truly, those who support evil by proclaiming that "God told me to. . ." have had no real conversation with our "One and only God", for God's love abides in all and evil has no part in God's love. When bad things happen, whether from our own choices, choices of others, or even unexplained, with God's guidance, we are provided the strength to overcome and become an inspiration to others.

I grieve for the "supposed" atheist. Since all people are given the "Light of God" within their souls, which are truly a gift and made in the image of God, it is a personal tragedy that they have found no avenue to honor Him, for their lives most surely lack true joy.

Perhaps they feel so successful "by themselves" that they have no need for God's guidance. In time, perhaps only in the end, they will have a need that only God the Father can meet and it is then they will recognize him; but sadly, their earthly lives have missed true joy!

Thomas stated that Jesus revealed that the coming of the Kingdom of God is not only coming but is already here, a continuing spiritual reality and that the living Jesus even challenged those who believe the Kingdom of God is in another place or even a future event, e.g.:

> *"What you look forever to, you do not recognize it, it is all around you."*

Thomas goes on to say:

> *"that without spiritual intuition, people grow old without joy. . . and die. . . without knowing God."*

In other words, we either discover the "Light" within or we live in darkness. There is no true joy in the life of the Atheist—life without God is an empty existence!

Thus, regarding the eternal journey of our souls, it seems fairly clear to me that when our earthly body ends its existence, God takes our soul home with him, *restores* it through rest, and then at his choosing, returns it to the family to continue his purpose. The 23rd Psalm, which is beloved by many, states:

> *"The Lord is my shepherd,*
> *I shall not want;*
> *He makes me to lie down in green*
> *pastures;*
> *He leads me beside still waters;*
> ***He restores my soul.***"

The Gospel of Thomas also lends support and clarification to my Presbyterian upbringing and belief in "predestination". Many misinterpret this to mean that God simply places his hand on our head and steers us throughout life—that we have no need to use our mind, to live the teachings of Christ—simply stand around and wait for "Him" to act. The true meaning is simply what is stated in this book: That when we take our first breath, God gives us a soul made in his image, to cherish, and with his guidance, his purpose for our soul will continue throughout our lives.

So,

> ***"Love the Lord your God with all your heart, with all your mind, and with all your soul, and and your neighbor as yourself".***

That's it! If we do that, God will take care of the rest!

Thomas describes how Jesus, prior to his arrest, held the hands of his disciples and asked them to dance with him. I believe that Christ was setting the example for all of us—that death is a time of celebration because he has given to all of us God's eternal "light" and we must celebrate one's life with joy!

I love to sing this beautiful hymn on that subject:

"They cut me down and I leapt up high,
I am the life that will never, never die;
I'll live in you, if you'll live in me;
I am the Lord of the dance, said he.

Dance, then, wherever you may be,
I am the Lord of the dance, said he;
And I'll lead you all wherever you may be,
And I'll lead you all in the dance, said
he."

EPILOGUE

When Paul was treated abusively for his preaching, the Lord came to him and in a vision said: "Do not be afraid, keep on speaking, do not be silent, for I am with you".

(Acts, 18:5 & 9)

When, in 1995, I completed my four books of "Threads" (the histories of my parents and my husband's parents), I believed that my writings were complete. However, about five years ago, I began to "feel" that there was still a book to be written. I was unable to identify it until this past year and with prayerful guidance, this is that book! To protect these words from the thoughts of others, I shared them with no one, not even my husband, to be sure that they conveyed only my personal journey.

When I questioned myself as to the importance of this story, I decided why not? After all, many books have been written about earthly journeys and explorations that inspired others to travel in their footsteps. Is this spiritual journey not just as spectacular?

Regardless of what our daily lives require of us, all are equally important to God's purpose and the pathway He has given each is personal and known only to Him. Thus, it is my prayer that this story will inspire others to take this journey and discover their own pathway, for it too is filled with awesome beauty and glory!

REFERENCES

Barthel, Manfred: The Jesuits: History and Legend of the Society of Jesus. New York: William Morrow, 1982.

Barthel, Manfred: What the Bible Really Says. New York: Wing Books, 1982.

Miller: The Gift of Kindness. New York: Crowell and Co, 1905.

Pagels, Elaine: Beyond Belief: The Secret Gospel of Thomas. New York: Random House, 2003

Tillerson, Patty P.: Threads, Book I: The History of Emma McInnis. (Unpublished, 1991). Copies provided to the Mormon Geneology Library, Salt Lake City and the Clayton Geneology Library, Houston, Texas.

Tillerson, Patty P: Threads, Book II: The History of Ray Vernon Patton. (Unpublished, 1992) Copies provided to the Mormon

Geneology Library, Salt Lake City and the Clayton Geneology Library, Houston, Texas.

About the Author

Having lost both her parents early in life, she felt much was denied her children in not knowing them. To fill this void, her prayers for guidance led her to develop a personal philosophy that, in turn, led her to write four books entitled "Threads" in which she based the histories of their four grandparents upon the religious practice of each. Over the past few years, she became aware that there was another book to be written and was amazed when, in reading the translations of the Secret Gospel of Thomas, how very much God had guided her early writings and thus, the book that was yet to be written is this one, "Eternal Threads."

Printed in the United States
35675LVS00002BA/59

9 781420 833515